teacher.

COMMUNICATION LOGBOOK

©The Life Graduate Publishing Group

No part of this book may be scanned, reproduced or distributed in any printed or electronic form without the prior permission of the author or publisher.

Education Planning Series

NAME _____

SCHOOL _____

YEAR _____

CONTACT INFORMATION

STUDENT NAME

D.O.B

Parent Name - Mother

Contact Phone No.

Contact Email

Parent Name - Father

Contact Phone No.

Contact Email

Emergency Contact #1 - Name & Relationship

Contact Phone No.

Emergency Contact #2 - Name & Relationship

Contact Phone No.

Medical Information

Other Details and Information

CONTACT INFORMATION

STUDENT NAME

D.O.B

Parent Name - Mother

Contact Phone No.

Contact Email

Parent Name - Father

Contact Phone No.

Contact Email

Emergency Contact #1 - Name & Relationship   Contact Phone No.

Emergency Contact #2 - Name & Relationship   Contact Phone No.

Medical Information

Other Details and Information

CONTACT INFORMATION

STUDENT NAME

D.O.B

Parent Name - Mother

Contact Phone No.

Contact Email

Parent Name - Father

Contact Phone No.

Contact Email

Emergency Contact #1 - Name & Relationship   Contact Phone No.

Emergency Contact #2 - Name & Relationship   Contact Phone No.

Medical Information

Other Details and Information

CONTACT INFORMATION

STUDENT NAME

D.O.B

Parent Name - Mother

Contact Phone No.

Contact Email

Parent Name - Father

Contact Phone No.

Contact Email

Emergency Contact #1 - Name & Relationship   Contact Phone No.

Emergency Contact #2 - Name & Relationship   Contact Phone No.

Medical Information

Other Details and Information

CONTACT INFORMATION

STUDENT NAME

D.O.B

Parent Name - Mother

Contact Phone No.

Contact Email

Parent Name - Father

Contact Phone No.

Contact Email

Emergency Contact #1 - Name & Relationship   Contact Phone No.

Emergency Contact #2 - Name & Relationship   Contact Phone No.

Medical Information

Other Details and Information

CONTACT INFORMATION

STUDENT NAME

D.O.B

Parent Name - Mother

Contact Phone No.

Contact Email

Parent Name - Father

Contact Phone No.

Contact Email

Emergency Contact #1 - Name & Relationship   Contact Phone No.

Emergency Contact #2 - Name & Relationship   Contact Phone No.

Medical Information

Other Details and Information

CONTACT INFORMATION

STUDENT NAME

D.O.B

Parent Name - Mother

Contact Phone No.

Contact Email

Parent Name - Father

Contact Phone No.

Contact Email

Emergency Contact #1 - Name & Relationship   Contact Phone No.

Emergency Contact #2 - Name & Relationship   Contact Phone No.

Medical Information

Other Details and Information

CONTACT INFORMATION

STUDENT NAME

D.O.B

Parent Name - Mother

Contact Phone No.

Contact Email

Parent Name - Father

Contact Phone No.

Contact Email

Emergency Contact #1 - Name & Relationship   Contact Phone No.

Emergency Contact #2 - Name & Relationship   Contact Phone No.

Medical Information

Other Details and Information

CONTACT INFORMATION

STUDENT NAME

D.O.B

Parent Name - Mother

Contact Phone No.

Contact Email

Parent Name - Father

Contact Phone No.

Contact Email

Emergency Contact #1 - Name & Relationship   Contact Phone No.

Emergency Contact #2 - Name & Relationship   Contact Phone No.

Medical Information

Other Details and Information

CONTACT INFORMATION

STUDENT NAME

D.O.B

Parent Name - Mother

Contact Phone No.

Contact Email

Parent Name - Father

Contact Phone No.

Contact Email

Emergency Contact #1 - Name & Relationship   Contact Phone No.

Emergency Contact #2 - Name & Relationship   Contact Phone No.

Medical Information

Other Details and Information

CONTACT INFORMATION

STUDENT NAME

D.O.B

Parent Name - Mother

Contact Phone No.

Contact Email

Parent Name - Father

Contact Phone No.

Contact Email

Emergency Contact #1 - Name & Relationship   Contact Phone No.

Emergency Contact #2 - Name & Relationship   Contact Phone No.

Medical Information

Other Details and Information

CONTACT INFORMATION

STUDENT NAME

D.O.B

Parent Name - Mother

Contact Phone No.

Contact Email

Parent Name - Father

Contact Phone No.

Contact Email

Emergency Contact #1 - Name & Relationship   Contact Phone No.

Emergency Contact #2 - Name & Relationship   Contact Phone No.

Medical Information

Other Details and Information

CONTACT INFORMATION

STUDENT NAME

D.O.B

Parent Name - Mother

Contact Phone No.

Contact Email

Parent Name - Father

Contact Phone No.

Contact Email

Emergency Contact #1 - Name & Relationship   Contact Phone No.

Emergency Contact #2 - Name & Relationship   Contact Phone No.

Medical Information

Other Details and Information

CONTACT INFORMATION

STUDENT NAME

D.O.B

Parent Name - Mother

Contact Phone No.

Contact Email

Parent Name - Father

Contact Phone No.

Contact Email

Emergency Contact #1 - Name & Relationship   Contact Phone No.

Emergency Contact #2 - Name & Relationship   Contact Phone No.

Medical Information

Other Details and Information

🏫 CONTACT INFORMATION

STUDENT NAME

D.O.B

Parent Name - Mother

Contact Phone No.

Contact Email

Parent Name - Father

Contact Phone No.

Contact Email

Emergency Contact #1 - Name & Relationship   Contact Phone No.

Emergency Contact #2 - Name & Relationship   Contact Phone No.

Medical Information

Other Details and Information

CONTACT INFORMATION

STUDENT NAME

D.O.B

Parent Name - Mother

Contact Phone No.

Contact Email

Parent Name - Father

Contact Phone No.

Contact Email

Emergency Contact #1 - Name & Relationship | Contact Phone No.

Emergency Contact #2 - Name & Relationship | Contact Phone No.

Medical Information

Other Details and Information

CONTACT INFORMATION

STUDENT NAME

D.O.B

Parent Name - Mother

Contact Phone No.

Contact Email

Parent Name - Father

Contact Phone No.

Contact Email

Emergency Contact #1 - Name & Relationship   Contact Phone No.

Emergency Contact #2 - Name & Relationship   Contact Phone No.

Medical Information

Other Details and Information

CONTACT INFORMATION

STUDENT NAME

D.O.B

Parent Name - Mother

Contact Phone No.

Contact Email

Parent Name - Father

Contact Phone No.

Contact Email

Emergency Contact #1 - Name & Relationship   Contact Phone No.

Emergency Contact #2 - Name & Relationship   Contact Phone No.

Medical Information

Other Details and Information

CONTACT INFORMATION

STUDENT NAME

D.O.B

Parent Name - Mother

Contact Phone No.

Contact Email

Parent Name - Father

Contact Phone No.

Contact Email

Emergency Contact #1 - Name & Relationship   Contact Phone No.

Emergency Contact #2 - Name & Relationship   Contact Phone No.

Medical Information

Other Details and Information

CONTACT INFORMATION

STUDENT NAME

D.O.B

Parent Name - Mother

Contact Phone No.

Contact Email

Parent Name - Father

Contact Phone No.

Contact Email

Emergency Contact #1 - Name & Relationship   Contact Phone No.

Emergency Contact #2 - Name & Relationship   Contact Phone No.

Medical Information

Other Details and Information

CONTACT INFORMATION

STUDENT NAME

D.O.B

Parent Name - Mother

Contact Phone No.

Contact Email

Parent Name - Father

Contact Phone No.

Contact Email

Emergency Contact #1 - Name & Relationship   Contact Phone No.

Emergency Contact #2 - Name & Relationship   Contact Phone No.

Medical Information

Other Details and Information

CONTACT INFORMATION

STUDENT NAME

D.O.B

Parent Name - Mother

Contact Phone No.

Contact Email

Parent Name - Father

Contact Phone No.

Contact Email

Emergency Contact #1 - Name & Relationship   Contact Phone No.

Emergency Contact #2 - Name & Relationship   Contact Phone No.

Medical Information

Other Details and Information

CONTACT INFORMATION

STUDENT NAME

D.O.B

Parent Name - Mother

Contact Phone No.

Contact Email

Parent Name - Father

Contact Phone No.

Contact Email

Emergency Contact #1 - Name & Relationship   Contact Phone No.

Emergency Contact #2 - Name & Relationship   Contact Phone No.

Medical Information

Other Details and Information

CONTACT INFORMATION

STUDENT NAME

D.O.B

Parent Name - Mother

Contact Phone No.

Contact Email

Parent Name - Father

Contact Phone No.

Contact Email

Emergency Contact #1 - Name & Relationship   Contact Phone No.

Emergency Contact #2 - Name & Relationship   Contact Phone No.

Medical Information

Other Details and Information

CONTACT INFORMATION

STUDENT NAME

D.O.B

Parent Name - Mother

Contact Phone No.

Contact Email

Parent Name - Father

Contact Phone No.

Contact Email

Emergency Contact #1 - Name & Relationship   Contact Phone No.

Emergency Contact #2 - Name & Relationship   Contact Phone No.

Medical Information

Other Details and Information

CONTACT INFORMATION

STUDENT NAME

D.O.B

Parent Name - Mother

Contact Phone No.

Contact Email

Parent Name - Father

Contact Phone No.

Contact Email

Emergency Contact #1 - Name & Relationship Contact Phone No.

Emergency Contact #2 - Name & Relationship Contact Phone No.

Medical Information

Other Details and Information

CONTACT INFORMATION

STUDENT NAME

D.O.B

Parent Name - Mother

Contact Phone No.

Contact Email

Parent Name - Father

Contact Phone No.

Contact Email

Emergency Contact #1 - Name & Relationship   Contact Phone No.

Emergency Contact #2 - Name & Relationship   Contact Phone No.

Medical Information

Other Details and Information

CONTACT INFORMATION

STUDENT NAME

D.O.B

Parent Name - Mother

Contact Phone No.

Contact Email

Parent Name - Father

Contact Phone No.

Contact Email

Emergency Contact #1 - Name & Relationship   Contact Phone No.

Emergency Contact #2 - Name & Relationship   Contact Phone No.

Medical Information

Other Details and Information

CONTACT INFORMATION

STUDENT NAME

D.O.B

Parent Name - Mother

Contact Phone No.

Contact Email

Parent Name - Father

Contact Phone No.

Contact Email

Emergency Contact #1 - Name & Relationship   Contact Phone No.

Emergency Contact #2 - Name & Relationship   Contact Phone No.

Medical Information

Other Details and Information

CONTACT INFORMATION

STUDENT NAME

D.O.B

Parent Name - Mother

Contact Phone No.

Contact Email

Parent Name - Father

Contact Phone No.

Contact Email

Emergency Contact #1 - Name & Relationship

Contact Phone No.

Emergency Contact #2 - Name & Relationship

Contact Phone No.

Medical Information

Other Details and Information

CONTACT INFORMATION

STUDENT NAME

D.O.B

Parent Name - Mother

Contact Phone No.

Contact Email

Parent Name - Father

Contact Phone No.

Contact Email

Emergency Contact #1 - Name & Relationship   Contact Phone No.

Emergency Contact #2 - Name & Relationship   Contact Phone No.

Medical Information

Other Details and Information

CONTACT INFORMATION

STUDENT NAME

D.O.B

Parent Name - Mother

Contact Phone No.

Contact Email

Parent Name - Father

Contact Phone No.

Contact Email

Emergency Contact #1 - Name & Relationship   Contact Phone No.

Emergency Contact #2 - Name & Relationship   Contact Phone No.

Medical Information

Other Details and Information

CONTACT INFORMATION

STUDENT NAME

D.O.B

Parent Name - Mother

Contact Phone No.

Contact Email

Parent Name - Father

Contact Phone No.

Contact Email

Emergency Contact #1 - Name & Relationship   Contact Phone No.

Emergency Contact #2 - Name & Relationship   Contact Phone No.

Medical Information

Other Details and Information

CONTACT INFORMATION

STUDENT NAME

D.O.B

Parent Name - Mother

Contact Phone No.

Contact Email

Parent Name - Father

Contact Phone No.

Contact Email

Emergency Contact #1 - Name & Relationship   Contact Phone No.

Emergency Contact #2 - Name & Relationship   Contact Phone No.

Medical Information

Other Details and Information

CONTACT INFORMATION

STUDENT NAME

D.O.B

Parent Name - Mother

Contact Phone No.

Contact Email

Parent Name - Father

Contact Phone No.

Contact Email

Emergency Contact #1 - Name & Relationship   Contact Phone No.

Emergency Contact #2 - Name & Relationship   Contact Phone No.

Medical Information

Other Details and Information

CONTACT INFORMATION

STUDENT NAME

D.O.B

Parent Name - Mother

Contact Phone No.

Contact Email

Parent Name - Father

Contact Phone No.

Contact Email

Emergency Contact #1 - Name & Relationship   Contact Phone No.

Emergency Contact #2 - Name & Relationship   Contact Phone No.

Medical Information

Other Details and Information

CONTACT INFORMATION

STUDENT NAME

D.O.B

Parent Name - Mother

Contact Phone No.

Contact Email

Parent Name - Father

Contact Phone No.

Contact Email

Emergency Contact #1 - Name & Relationship   Contact Phone No.

Emergency Contact #2 - Name & Relationship   Contact Phone No.

Medical Information

Other Details and Information

CONTACT INFORMATION

STUDENT NAME

D.O.B

Parent Name - Mother

Contact Phone No.

Contact Email

Parent Name - Father

Contact Phone No.

Contact Email

Emergency Contact #1 - Name & Relationship   Contact Phone No.

Emergency Contact #2 - Name & Relationship   Contact Phone No.

Medical Information

Other Details and Information

CONTACT INFORMATION

STUDENT NAME

D.O.B

Parent Name - Mother

Contact Phone No.

Contact Email

Parent Name - Father

Contact Phone No.

Contact Email

Emergency Contact #1 - Name & Relationship   Contact Phone No.

Emergency Contact #2 - Name & Relationship   Contact Phone No.

Medical Information

Other Details and Information

CONTACT INFORMATION

STUDENT NAME

D.O.B

Parent Name - Mother

Contact Phone No.

Contact Email

Parent Name - Father

Contact Phone No.

Contact Email

Emergency Contact #1 - Name & Relationship　　Contact Phone No.

Emergency Contact #2 - Name & Relationship　　Contact Phone No.

Medical Information

Other Details and Information

CONTACT INFORMATION

STUDENT NAME

D.O.B

Parent Name - Mother

Contact Phone No.

Contact Email

Parent Name - Father

Contact Phone No.

Contact Email

Emergency Contact #1 - Name & Relationship   Contact Phone No.

Emergency Contact #2 - Name & Relationship   Contact Phone No.

Medical Information

Other Details and Information

CONTACT INFORMATION

STUDENT NAME

D.O.B

Parent Name - Mother

Contact Phone No.

Contact Email

Parent Name - Father

Contact Phone No.

Contact Email

Emergency Contact #1 - Name & Relationship   Contact Phone No.

Emergency Contact #2 - Name & Relationship   Contact Phone No.

Medical Information

Other Details and Information

CONTACT INFORMATION

STUDENT NAME

D.O.B

Parent Name - Mother

Contact Phone No.

Contact Email

Parent Name - Father

Contact Phone No.

Contact Email

Emergency Contact #1 - Name & Relationship   Contact Phone No.

Emergency Contact #2 - Name & Relationship   Contact Phone No.

Medical Information

Other Details and Information

CONTACT INFORMATION

STUDENT NAME

D.O.B

Parent Name - Mother

Contact Phone No.

Contact Email

Parent Name - Father

Contact Phone No.

Contact Email

Emergency Contact #1 - Name & Relationship   Contact Phone No.

Emergency Contact #2 - Name & Relationship   Contact Phone No.

Medical Information

Other Details and Information

CONTACT INFORMATION

STUDENT NAME

D.O.B

Parent Name - Mother

Contact Phone No.

Contact Email

Parent Name - Father

Contact Phone No.

Contact Email

Emergency Contact #1 - Name & Relationship   Contact Phone No.

Emergency Contact #2 - Name & Relationship   Contact Phone No.

Medical Information

Other Details and Information

CONTACT INFORMATION

STUDENT NAME

D.O.B

Parent Name - Mother

Contact Phone No.

Contact Email

Parent Name - Father

Contact Phone No.

Contact Email

Emergency Contact #1 - Name & Relationship | Contact Phone No.

Emergency Contact #2 - Name & Relationship | Contact Phone No.

Medical Information

Other Details and Information

CONTACT INFORMATION

STUDENT NAME

D.O.B

Parent Name - Mother

Contact Phone No.

Contact Email

Parent Name - Father

Contact Phone No.

Contact Email

Emergency Contact #1 - Name & Relationship   Contact Phone No.

Emergency Contact #2 - Name & Relationship   Contact Phone No.

Medical Information

Other Details and Information

CONTACT INFORMATION

STUDENT NAME

D.O.B

Parent Name - Mother

Contact Phone No.

Contact Email

Parent Name - Father

Contact Phone No.

Contact Email

Emergency Contact #1 - Name & Relationship   Contact Phone No.

Emergency Contact #2 - Name & Relationship   Contact Phone No.

Medical Information

Other Details and Information

CONTACT INFORMATION

STUDENT NAME

D.O.B

Parent Name - Mother

Contact Phone No.

Contact Email

Parent Name - Father

Contact Phone No.

Contact Email

Emergency Contact #1 - Name & Relationship   Contact Phone No.

Emergency Contact #2 - Name & Relationship   Contact Phone No.

Medical Information

Other Details and Information

CONTACT INFORMATION

STUDENT NAME

D.O.B

Parent Name - Mother

Contact Phone No.

Contact Email

Parent Name - Father

Contact Phone No.

Contact Email

Emergency Contact #1 - Name & Relationship   Contact Phone No.

Emergency Contact #2 - Name & Relationship   Contact Phone No.

Medical Information

Other Details and Information

CONTACT INFORMATION

STUDENT NAME

D.O.B

Parent Name - Mother

Contact Phone No.

Contact Email

Parent Name - Father

Contact Phone No.

Contact Email

Emergency Contact #1 - Name & Relationship   Contact Phone No.

Emergency Contact #2 - Name & Relationship   Contact Phone No.

Medical Information

Other Details and Information

CONTACT INFORMATION

STUDENT NAME

D.O.B

Parent Name - Mother

Contact Phone No.

Contact Email

Parent Name - Father

Contact Phone No.

Contact Email

Emergency Contact #1 - Name & Relationship | Contact Phone No.

Emergency Contact #2 - Name & Relationship | Contact Phone No.

Medical Information

Other Details and Information

teacher.

COMMUNICATION LOGBOOK

www.ingramcontent.com/pod-product-compliance
Lightning Source LLC
LaVergne TN
LVHW060141080526
838202LV00049B/4052